RANGI CHANGI
AND OTHER POEMS

*To Jo
With Very Best Wishes*

RANGI CHANGI
AND OTHER POEMS

Malcolm Carson

*Malcolm Carson
6-X-2011*

Shoestring Press

All rights reserved. No part of this work covered by the copyright hereon may be reproduced or used in any means – graphic, electronic, or mechanical, including copying, recording, taping, or information storage and retrieval systems – without written permission of the publisher.

Printed by imprintdigital
Upton Pyne, Exeter
www.imprintdigital.net

Typeset by Nathanael Ravenlock
nat@ravenlock.eu

Published by Shoestring Press
19 Devonshire Avenue, Beeston, Nottingham, NG9 1BS
(0115) 925 1827
www.shoestringpress.co.uk

First published 2010
© Copyright: Malcolm Carson
The moral right of the author has been asserted.
ISBN 978 1 907356 18 6

ACKNOWLEDGEMENTS

Acknowledgements are due to the editors of the following where versions of some of the poems have previously appeared: *Other Poetry, The Bow-Wow Shop, Big Little Poems, iota, The Coffee House*.

Some poems in the *Rangi Changi* sequence have previously appeared in a limited edition with the same name published by Eyelet Press in 2009.

For my sons:

Conor, Declan and Dillon Carson

Contents

GY	1
S. Freud, Fish Merchant	3
Starfish	5
St Stephen's Day	6
Wheelings	7
Ralph's Jacket	8
Migration	9
Occasional visit	10
Title deeds	11
Demesnes	13

Rangi Changi

Kathmandu	17
The climb	18
The teacher	19
Terraces	20
Bird spotting	21
Innocence and Experience	22
The Maoists	23
The Myna bird	24
Rangi changi	25
Inside the Tea-house	26
The Wren	27
In the Sanctuary	28
Coming down	30
Bamboo	31
Chomrong	32
Pokhara	33
Hotel Himalaya	35

Gelt Woods	39
Jay	41
Magpie	42
Buzzard	43
Winter solstice	44
Wren	45
Local woman marries Death Row prisoner	46
The Peasants of Flagey	47
Thomas Bewick in Ovingham church	49
In the Café Franz Kafka	50
Edgar sits by the Eden	51
Edgar refuses marriage	52
Edgar is happy	53
Edgar in winter	54
Edgar considers a mortgage	55
Edgar by the Gelt	56
Edgar takes an allotment	58

GY

"I've never been" they say "no need"
to that flat town where land smudges
to the sea. Some though pass through
in their migrations, make their mark elsewhere.
Grim at least gave his name, stayed
long enough to save Havelock the Dane.
Freud stepped ashore, passed on
to find Lancashire's horrors were enough
to make him hoy his dafter themes.
Jazzmen have played, great poets
in those dreary pubs ringing
out against the Humber's fog.
B. S. Johnson came, the 'pleasure tripper',
took a trip, felt sick a lot, wrote The Trawl.

Most though know their home,
horizons of the Wolds and Spurn,
Dock Tower's finger that points to
when fishermen would weigh their lives
with dock gates' opening, closing.
Trips pulsed with violence, drawing wealth
from turbulent depths: frozen warps
baroque with ice, crushing trawl gates,
thunder of engine, silver of haul.
Then docked again, big suit each trip,
love bought and dutiful, strut through
the pubs of Freeman Street,
fights as big as Iceland.

Clogs on pavements would scrape my sleep,
the dull reassurance of the estuary bell
answering the fog horns' complaints,
cavalier helmets of the smoking houses
that snapped to the wind's directives.
Bikes by battalions at the dock gates
marshalled for smuggled haddock, plaice –
cod was for Yorkies.
The parcel of fish on our doorstep Fridays,
for the ref. too at Blundell Park.
Barter in the pubs – dock for allotment –
in sack bags that swung from
unsteady handlebars.
                    Then quotas,
wars, idleness that corroded boats and hearts.

We've seen him countless times
close his car, look round, concerned
– television cameras – walk towards the house,
the Caretaker's, close it to our understanding.
Now it's crushed to ballast
like all the lives he's visited
in seeking after self.

Others have turned the rusting knife
that gutted the glistening shoals
upon their own. Infected in the gill
they slobber in the dying current,
the standing pools, contaminate
river and worthy port where at least
some sorts of violence could be understood.

S. Freud, Fish Merchant

In July 1875, Sigmund Freud, aged 19, disembarked at Grimsby from Bremerhaven on his way to Manchester. He might have stayed longer…

The touch of her finger was enough,
my life decided beneath the table
at the welcoming dinner, a charge of delight
such as I had never known.
Our eyes had met, and when we were seated
side by side, I sweated with desire.

I only should have stayed the day
en route to Manchester but found
I could not part, all thoughts
of my career usurped by passion.
Did I betray you, Amalia, dear mother,
in submitting to desires I should suppress?
I dream of you still, of what might have been,
know Breuer, Charcot, Brücke,
make advances where
I might have led, where I could have
laid out all before a gawping world.
The touch, though, of her finger was enough.

Should I have known, sailing up
the muddy Humber towards
the beckoning tower of Grimsby that
I would be netted in such currents
which swirl and eddy in our unconscious?
The lodestar of her beauty drew me on
to banks. Now my life is silted with

the business of fish. Her father
took me on but soon my patience
with his possessiveness wore thin;
I said that in his house my wife should only be a guest,
defer to me in all things. And so, mama,
you see there's room still for you.

I know my fish – haddock, plaice
precious skate, lesser cod, lascivious halibut
– can bid at auction, know the cuts to make,
how long to ice and where to sell.
Perhaps I'm seen by some as strange;
my accent, manners may stand out
on early morning markets
on the slow-rocking pontoon. No matter
for they come to me with their troubles,
this foreigner whose hands stink of what they know.
The wives especially, hysterical, repressed,
transfer affection to the one who listens,
who knows the price of fish, the cost of passion.

Starfish

One we saw with excitement,
then others, until we knew
here was death on a grand scale.
Galaxies of starfish corpsed
between breakwaters, indecently
pink and naked: *Asteroidea*
swept out of their firmament
to our prurient gaze.
Surfeited we turned to driftwood,
pallets, bath rings of coal,
the estuary's economy: decent
stuff, what we might expect
from a clattering tide.
Heavy ponies promenade over
the corrugated sand, a brushmark away
from rusting forts, Spurn's lighthouse.
Sea gathers to fatten through creeks
slides to the margin where the starfish lie,
touches, pulls back.

St Stephen's Day

Irby Dale, Lincolnshire

They have corridored these hills,
this valley, against the leisure seekers.
Barbed wire now charts the options
where limestone crags crumble
against the wind.

It's the year's end and haws blacken
on the thorn bush greening in the lea.
Blackbirds know I'm here as does the wren
which once was hunted on this day,
sticks beating it out of its cave of song.

I lean against the gate,
look down the field of kale,
watch pigeons homing. A flock
of greenfinches takes off
from the ash carrying its shape,
trills across the valley
settles on another.
Against the odds a robin sings
while crows caw antiphony.

Wheelings

We called it lunch, drawn to the barn's warmth
from hay bales steaming primeval sweat.
We'd unfold our fare, tractors idling
the day's steady pulse, waiting. Waiting
too, the rats, uneasy, this their domain,
resentment in their scuttle, hump of back,
sinister tail, while with cow muck on our hands
scented with diesel, we ate. We yarned like travellers as though
oceans were our only bounds, instead
of parishes, the constant drum from hill to field,
wheelings ever deeper patterning our days.

We returned to our cabs and spreaders, baler band
hanging like severed sinews, blades
battered by crewyard stones. Before we went
we'd fling a fork at a rat or two. Sometimes
we'd skewer one, let them know who's boss.

Ralph's Jacket

That last summer you sat together, soft
in talk across the years. He told you secrets
in the sun, opened up the darkest
hours of disappointment and regret

just as a boy remembers the broken nest
– an expiation of a kind. In the greenhouse
tomatoes ripened, chrysanthemums
billowed, geraniums spilt scarlet to the floor

slatted with shadows where woodlice shuffled. He'd
housepainters round while weather permitted, that window
put right at last, had settled up accounts
and smiled.
Now hot from my climb I fold

his jacket that you gave me, a pillow among
the heather high above Kirkstone Pass.
A quirky weave of continuities, this,
catching up the days of myth, errant
paths across the fells and his sad parting.

Migration

Beyond the sad resort birds intent
over corrugated sand, harried by a tide
that creeps among the thorny marsh,
creeps, and catches unawares. Geese,
turnstones, oystercatchers, curlew, maddened redshank
that chink alarm in leggy flight.
                                    October.
Binoculars water in our eyes, forts
rust, river swells, freighters wait
at Humber mouth for tide to turn.
Cod line buoys draw taut like the skyline
low in its huge heaven.
                         As sure as Spurn's lighthouse
needles the east we come each year.
We straddle the beach like strings of wrack,
tread shells, haul at fish boxes.
Like the birds we ratch in the sand, for what,
we cannot tell, but know somehow
the timing of our leaving and arriving.

Occasional visit

We visit still the town
and mean to tend the grave
but often as not
don't. And when we do
the boys place flowers
and are sad. We clean
the stones, shake out our memories.
They scurry after squirrels
while we read inscriptions
for fishing worthies, Polish émigrés,
then saunter out.

I expected more at first
as though a burial place
might tell me things that I
had left behind or if remembered
had only seen as fleeting.
But no. Visiting is this
for us, and will mean less
for them until a curiosity
at best for parish hagiographers.

Title deeds

In my peculiar dreams
you have changed the locks
of houses that once were mine.

You have parked your caravan
tipped out your handbag
of furniture and family on the floor.

You have gilded rooms with your taste,
made the garden to your grand design,
usurped my station by the hearth.

But don't imagine I haven't a key
to what you now believe is yours, secure.
For in my recalcitrant dreams

I inhabit your houses again
– I choose not to call them home
as that's still mine to name.

Letting in my cats we lie down
in beds that still are ours,
make tea, attend to gardens

that evidently you've not understood.
Cats will scrat and nudge
their way to nest in familiar chairs.

In all we'll settle while you're out,
see you as tenants but
should you appear we'll make our excuses.

Then, in my turn, I can't be sure
who looks from our own windows,
scoffs at what they find,

sighs at memories, lost loves,
dry hearts, before silently
closing their dreams behind them.

Demesnes

She took possession
of the Ward's estate –
tubs of lobelia, geraniums
on the orderly patio – set out
chairs obedient to her.
Rhythms to be danced to
even here where seasons
are suspended in
a fog of dependence.
'Like seals,' she said of others,
'waiting for fish.'
Around herself she put up
a palisade – *Mansfield Park*,
Elective Affinities, her geniality,
her knowingness.
Letting others patronise
she offered forbearance
to their familiarity.
Talk of her house, though,
and what next drew her
beneath a carapace
of remembered stories,
her eyes fading to
a clouded distance
black hours of comas
and the narrowing of precincts.

RANGI CHANGI

Kathmandu

Pick up the rhythms, slow step out
into traffic that honks at itself,
walk as surely as these cows
that lumber in holiness
beside the Mercedes ads.

This city grows like a puddle in dust,
flooding the weakest spots.
Kites in flocks above the hillside
wait for cadavers, mewing above
the cars' cacophony,
chatter of monkeys grooming beneath
telegraphs of prayer flags,
the trundling prayer wheels.
Such diligence of hope.

Steal yourself against the beggars,
tell the usual tales that let us off
before we haggle for pence,
taxis and the usual stuff,
leave the monkeys being thwacked
by women with besoms
that sweep away our passing steps.

The climb

Like Helvellyn this
up from Swirls
the steps that
regiment your pace
breathing
challenge
your rhythm thoughts
hands on knees the push
against yourself
body arched
embracing sweat
watching shadow
just ahead the porter's heels
though with your pack
and others'
puts you to shame
makes you push
and push listen
to your breath
scouring lungs
feels this good
to know it's like Hel-
vellyn up from Swirls.

The teacher

I met him on the roadside
just beyond the tea-house.
He talked about his job
in the village school
which he pointed out down
the valley. Told me selling
drinks to trekkers helped him
make ends meet, loved English
which he taught, wanted me
to say if he made mistakes,
here with the hawks overhead
unruly cattle being herded,
Machhapuchre beckoning.

When I think of Dhampus,
it's of him gathering what he could,
putting away carefully for winter
just as he did his stack of dried kindling.

Terraces

Ribbed beyond probability
they ratchet the eye down the valleys.
Odd houses are pegged along the line
where tillers planted their hopes
against the hillside's whimsies.
Close to, cabbages, corn
leeks, prosaic stuff,
a scatter of hens, lumbering buffalo,
but draw back and you see
an ancient script.

In the rain at Chomrong
the women still write with adze,
chinking against the wilful stones,
knowing a break from their squat
would mean less time to trap the rain,
would let it smudge for good
the pages of the family's history,
give it up for the monsoon's pulp.

Bird spotting

Kites were easy above the city
strung high over the monastery
scenting death in their lazy
pirouettes among the stinking thermals.

Once, above a tea-house, a hawk
begged identification, long enough
in my glasses – bright yellow bill,
white under the wings – obliging.

Landlady hated it for it snaffled
her chickens. Then there was
a Roller, I think, and a sort
of magpie in the bamboo,

no white or purple – I write from notes –
red and yellow finches,
a jungle myna that had learnt
a wolf-whistle from trekkers, perhaps.

We knew the eagles as we took drinks
by the thatched tea-house
where the buffalo sulked
and porters slapped stories down like cards.

I could have tried harder,
I suppose, have logged their songs,
their flight and colours of primaries,
secondaries, the way they sat,
their 'giz', but couldn't make
an inventory of my amazement.

Innocence and Experience

I went back to see the orchids
seeping from the rotting trunk
which hung over the trail
– white, delicate, muscular.
Poised to frame them, a girl came
into view, pagging her brother.
'Picture?' she said.
For them to see, I thought,
and swung the finder round
and snapped 'the colourful scene',
the native dress. Such technology,
they're sure to be impressed.
They gathered round the screen,
glanced a moment, then turned:
'Picture? Money?' Shocked,
I told them no and moved away,
her snarl the image I recall.

The Maoists

They marched through Landruk
certain of their chant, their banners,
small men, fierce and friendly,
wishing us 'Good morning', 'Namaste'.
The villagers stopped, uncertain,
knowing the recent past –
the beatings, sabotage, disappearances.
Out in the open now, election
in full swing, they smiled in rôle.

Halted on the steps to the river,
a leader enquired of me
amicably enough: 'Do you
support a free communist Nepal?'
Considering the implications of freedom
and communism in the context
of a feudal, monarchical,
medieval hegemony,
and what was meant by my support,
the answer was clear, immediate:
'Yes, of course!' Each satisfied,
he went on to govern,
I to wander by the Modi Khola,
work towards Annapurna's snows.

The Myna bird

Away from her stall of pigtailed hats,
bracelets, knitwear, necklaces –
displaced crafts of another place –
she sits with her basket of beads.

Singing to herself
she threads sad thoughts
in reds and yellows,
black, turquoise, silver clasps.

Then, sudden, like a myna bird,
she mimics what she hears:
Just looking; *C'est combien?*
and startles punters with themselves.

Caged in her dreams
she hoards the bits of language
as she does her beads,
brings them out as objets trouvés,
strings them together on a whim,
glossy, brilliant in the sun.

Rangi changi

Purple polyanthus precious in the mossy rocks
waymark us through the bamboo jungle.
A family of monkeys jabber
as they link across a flail of trees.
We stop, look up at rhododendron
flare red through green.
'Rangi changi!' says Nuri,
arms embracing the whole.
We agree, loving the sound,
not needing the meaning:
'Beautiful many-coloured landscape'.

For a moment I'm in
'a green thought in a green shade'
but here it's nature's gardeners
that draw this composition
renewing itself within a larger scheme.

Light down the valley softens into pink.
A dead tree is a silhouette, another growing from it
as does the orchid finding new growth in old.
Such endless growth on growth.
The valley is awash with rain finding cracks,
crevices, weaknesses, insistent.
Slabs of granite come alive, glisten silver
in the darkening hours.
Gorge narrows as first snow feathers the air
but still it's 'Rangi changi'.

Inside the Tea-house

Someone tries a radio.
Smoke from the kitchen
drifts over the rhododendrons.
A jangle of pans
as the floor blazes.
Laughter falls back
with the flames.
Rain syncopates
on corrugated roof
against the drum
of thunder in the gorge,
the river's continuo.
Light dims with the current
from the hydroelectric –
strange with the rain.
A Mona Lisa print
inscrutably on the wall
here below the gaunt
icy slabs of Machhapuchre.
Two women sit apart,
embroider, chatter, look up,
laugh, embroider. Porters,
guides, trekkers, hosts
– all stitched into this moment.

The Wren

Here you are again,
chivvying me
through the fresh snow,
each step a shiver of sweat,
a drink of breath.
I manage though
to say 'Hello' in your
slab of a cave.
You really are
Troglodytes troglodytes
as much as I saw you
on St. Stephen's Day
in Lincolnshire's grand emptiness,
or down my terrace at home
where you bickered at me
in my domestic husbandry.
Why do you follow me, wren,
with your 'tic-tic-tic',
your quizzical tail?
I'll do what I want, thank you,
as hard as this is
as foolish as I am, maybe,
and tomorrow I'm sure
you'll berate me again
ecstatic on Annapurna's slopes.

In the Sanctuary

Machhapuchre, Hiun Chuli,
Tharpa Chuli, Gangapurna,
Annapurna South, then III.

I learn to pronounce their names,
tick them off as you would
trains or a shopping list.

We stand and look, then stand
and look again as light
and cloud shift each peak

crevasse, each jutting rock
and brings it to our eye,
to be amazed, daunted.

Glaciers moan with weight
of expectation, avalanches
jag at the heart.

Astride our modest ridge
I mimic exploration,
pick a route that in my mind

will see me up to Annapurna,
zig-zag with the best
to reach that far arête

before the grand assault.
Though even this tightens breath
knowing my feeble grasp.

To be here is enough – that bolder
stuff is for other souls
who need to make an endless climb.

Mid-afternoon and clouds are closing
down the sun. Snow falls
on the Base Camp, miniature below

where there's a gathering of needs and hopes,
a braiding of histories before
time's fast unravelling.

Coming down

The odd boulder, irregular as breath
heaves through the brilliant snow.
The first this morning – the first ever,
it seems – we track along
a guessed-at contour
prodding as though in dark,
Mere playthings here, we dance
down through drifts, our yelps
of delight as we disappear
up to our oxters. As though
running for a bus, our guide
dashes his own route, umbrella
raised for 'the English party',
his glee as bright as the sun on snow
his disregard for duty leaping with each bound.

Too soon the forest. Branches
spring back, freed from weeping snow.
Tracks merge, compact, turn to slush, to mud.

Bamboo

We're in a Japanese print here
the air as fine as porcelain
taking breakfast at the teahouse.

The mist is lifting.
Sprays of bamboo are sketched
with a taut pencil

on the washed jungle slopes.
Placed, as we think, in the centre
our breath lifting with the mist

we speak our lines
while the Modi Khola runs
and birds articulate the trees.

Chomrong

As from the forest floor
the song breaks into bud,
slow, certain in the night air.
It runs from a single voice
and webs the throats
of the gathered throng,
surges into bloom,
pulsed by drummers.
From their midst a dancer emerges,
orchidaceous,
salutes the audience
then dances with the elegance of petals
demure, each movement
as sinuous as the turn of song.
Outrageous then the cock of the walk
who stomps around her
parodying her sweet restraint,
a rampant Chauntecleer,
hat skew-whiff, acrobatic
in his carnival, his burlesque of mating.
And like the maid enticed
but not submitting
she dances on, sublime,
her eyes and movement
seemingly untouched
yet knowing all too well
the part she'd play
in life's longer dance.

Pokhara

With religious diligence
he anoints my beard
in cream. Waits, prepares
the razor, towels, oils.

Cut-throat blade
slices through
the softened hair,
a clean page of face.

We talk to ease
the stroke of steel,
the strangeness
of my seated rôle.

And then the oils
that palpitate,
that rub me into glee,
buff away reserve.

This is Pokhara for me –
keen shave, bath,
tourist indulgences,
cars, thronged streets.

Some make of it
a staging post of hippy trails,
eager to gather to them
tales of border spats,

of fears of civil war,
their lives an endless quest
on roads that lead
to further roads.

Others gather for a wedding,
the bride and groom,
uneasy on an elephant
that knows too much.

Light draws back
as pashminas are herded
into bazaars, tills emptied
and pavements turn precarious.
Across the lake holy Machhapuchre
fades from view too soon.

Hotel Himalaya

Look out on to the lawn,
the perfect swimming pool
where the waiter attends
to a solitary bather
inclined beneath
the parasol, reading.
He returns to his station,
immaculate in movement,
at the Sports Club bar.

*

Watch the kites circle,
harried by crows,
as waiters prepare
the conference room:
chairs straightened, blotters
squared up, badges ready.
Around the borders, gardeners
crouch on haunches
chipping with adzes
at the solid ground drying
after the lawn sprinklers.

*

Listen to the loudspeakers
up the road to Patan,
urgent, shrilling
voters for tomorrow.

*

See the Japanese arrive,
the hotel lobby bulge
with trolleyed luggage,
orchid welcomes,
exaggerated bows,
happy cacophony above
the loop of easy listening.

*

Now to Patan,
avoid the open sewer
in the broken pavement,
past the mystery of motor bikes
queued outside the offices,
avoid the gaze
of batoned soldiers
marshalling the riders,
twitchy with elections.

*

Pass the rubbish in the side street
the medieval workshops
gaudy with gold Buddhas,
Ganeshas – a panoply of gods
for every taste.
The retriever pup slides
down the plastic liners,
where gutters silt
with the mulch of years.

*

To the square where
gods and temples, cars and cables,
bikes and offices – life's commerce –
have struck a deal.
Some find solace
in their meagre lot,
others in the shouted slogan,
the fervent banner, simplicities of hope.

Gelt Woods

I pulse up sandstone hills
through beeches, pines,
between the Gelt and sculpted quarry
where Romans scored their name,
now beneath a drape of moss
that drips its presence in sandy runs.
Red squirrels, keen to my breath, leap
leave me where wild garlic bruises the air
and the dipper dips in the river's delight.

I drop down, scent the deer
see its rump high in the sheen
of birches in the clearing
where the sun cracks open
the wood's kernel. I cough,
get up embarrassed for it,
give it the dignity of
a chase to the river.

A dormouse dares across
my path. I stoop amazed
at its temerity.

We swam in these dark pools
where the Gelt knuckles out
sandstone groins
beneath the hermit's cave.
Cold stripped our legs to bone.
We cried with pain
as simple as water.

I break my step for the goldcrest's chink
its flit between the pines
as light as its breath,
see treecreeper needle
up the pine, nuthatch down
making a perfect gyre.

I wonder should I look for more in this,
answer myself with running on
beyond reflection, touching bark
as I round trees, sensing trails
that giddy above the silver Gelt,
dancing over varicose roots
inhaling the gasp of the wood's heave.

Jay

Its shriek first
the claws in my hair
a battery of wings
about my head

knew how somehow
to invade from the dark
alders and oaks
by the Gelt.

My ear a chamber
of its cry that came
from the bole of the trees
the lichen the perished

waters the drum
of the seasons
that brought the woods
to their knowing.

Magpie

A flotsam hour between the tides of trains,
magpie has followed me down England's tracks
in pairs, unlucky threes and once in parliament.
Nuneaton now; perched in its siding on the ash,
scares off a stave of linnets who flute across
to seed heads on unlikely heap of stones.

I want to like you 'Margaret', try
Pica pica but to no avail,
admire your robes, episcopal, your jaunty
walk, Jack the lad. But go no further
for you've found your patch here where
you'll be Chauntecleer and glamorise
neglected sheds, your chatter the wisest words.

Buzzard

Felt its whoosh
a soft breeze
on my neck
heart's leap
turned, saw it climb
veer, hold steady
come again following
the fell's drop
helmeted.
Eyes meet
each feather flexed
for purpose.
Feet stumble over
heather, bilberry
a dance of panic
away cowering
beneath attack
again, again.
And then the run
towards the river
from its domain
out of its knowledge.

Winter solstice

It was the dipper's breast
flashing white
where the Gelt leaned into
sockets of sandstone,
the glint of crown
of goldcrest in the beech
in that last minute
in thickening gloom
which fixed this day for me.

Wren

Huge in song against the ash,
Troglodytes troglodytes,
angled tail and querying head,
it sees above that haze of flies
and forays out in rapid whirr,
fastidious diner of the air.
Huge in song against the ash
Troglodytes troglodytes.

Local woman marries Death Row prisoner

How they envy me that embrace
my moment of touch, smell, flex
of muscle, taste of saliva
the echo behind his eyes.
The camera tells a lie
for he clasps me still,
forever, my knowledge greater
than that of the one he killed.
Should I be jealous,
resent their time together
the knowledge of a life exhaled, replete?
Or is this the better way?
I have sucked his breath,
take it with me, breathe it in
when I will, consume it, know
his dependence, the myth
of his triumph in the clanging cell.
Our perspex love will blossom
with *Sweet Nothin's*. I have become
what I have always wanted,
have written my novella, victim and victor.
God! how I love him.

The Peasants of Flagey Returning from the Fair (Doubs)

after the painting by Gustave Courbet

Of course you don't like them
you mock and deride,
see as vulgar and ugly,
as coinage of pub signs,
or boards at fairs.
Lampoon my animals
'stuffed like *poupées*'
my friends 'mere mannequins',
in your *Journal de Rire*!

My father Régis, though,
rides whip in hand
into your Salon,
brings home his cows
scraggy for fattening,
wears his blue smock,
commands your attention,
like it or not.
'Perspective's not right,
spatial relationship,
each subject's detached.'
I know all about
your 'central authority'
in matters of taste.
I know too my rôle,
democrat, republican,

worker-painter,
a voice for the people
you scoff at.

They ride, my *campagnards*, or walk from the fair
with a purpose you choose to ignore,
these 'specimens of our mountain population'.
Better watch out! for that man with a pig tied by its hoof
will run round your ankles, will shit on your floor.

Thomas Bewick in Ovingham church

A sort of pilgrimage on my way from a meeting,
I found your headstone moved to the porch
sheltering from the softening rain.
I stood aside with you to let in the class of children
for a mock wedding, carried on my reading
of your epitaph, recalled what I knew
of your name – common enough round here –
amid the babble of ceremony, the caw of jackdaw
and the chatter of monuments.

You would have wanted this, I'm sure,
the peace of known patterns, the ordinariness
of death and life side by side, for how often
did they send you animals, birds, stuffed or shot,
and stinking fish to your door to revive
each hair, feather and scale, cut by precious cut?

In the Café Franz Kafka

I have ordered, and sit
obediently in a bentwood chair
which I selected from those available.
Each rocked but since so did the table
I settled for some syncopation.
I am to have coffee and cake.
I know the cost, know how
it fits in my budget. If
the service is good, I may
give some perquisite.
But time will tell.
               Dark
panelling, bare boards,
photographs of Siroka street
and of faces, drawn, severe. Familiar.

I am not challenged,
do not feel the need to defer.
This suits me so long as
all corresponds with
my sense of decorum,
is not tardy or profligate,
matches, in short, my tariff
of expectation. And should
by chance I forget my umbrella
neglect any crumbs down my front,
a cough or a *Sir* in the street
would befit my station.

Edgar sits by the Eden

Look for the kingfisher
see it stitch its silks
above the falls. Wait, wait…
it should come from among the willows.

See the salmon slob
in eddies. Who could curtail
such memory on the whim
of line's tug and tease?

Will the vole return
to banks where swanky mink
invade the commonwealth
of beasts and willow?

The balsam stinks so sweetly
above the nettles
and noble thistle, belies
its swelling armoury of seeds.

I mould the river
to my days, choose
a runnel of debate,
follow debris's swift demise.

Best like this, for too much
cogitation draws me down
to depths where sorrow lies.
I will bear free and patient thoughts.

Edgar refuses marriage

In Nahum Tate's 1681 reworking of *King Lear*, Edgar marries
Cordelia in order to effect a happy ending.

Why should he think to tear her from her father's arms
who looks in vain for mist on looking-glass?
How pluck her from that happy prison where
they would have laughed at lesser beings gad
round fortune's hooves like angry clegs? Does he think
we suffer less when happiness contrives
to dull our senses to the tempest in our hearts?

Ninny! Does he suppose I'll settle for
a salvaged fate, pretend I never was
on that heath, Poor Tom, was never called by Frateretto
or saw my father blinded by blind judgement's storm?
I'll not accept the solace of a truth
ignored, for then would Edgar be abused,
his marriage bed racked with barbs and blisters,
his coupling demented with the cries of bride
and groom for their gross betrayal.

I'll have none of it. Instead I'll clip the box
tend lavender, bruise the thyme on broken paths,
watch the heron, do such unrelated
things that never will amount to much,
that never will feed an ending to the fatuous crowd.

Edgar is happy

I am distracted from dark thoughts,
join in delight, despite myself,
at small birds that dink to my feeder.
Such a flutter of the soul.
Brazen chaffinch drops offerings
to his happy other, skirrs
to the hedge. Stately pigeon
lumps across the lawn
scouring for orts.
Woodpecker stabs its presence.
I could pick a diamond blade of grass to gaze on,
but am happy as I am for now.
I know that Frateretto may call
and Tom follow, that the foul fiend
lurks, but still this day at least
includes me in the parliament
of things glorious.

Edgar in winter

It's the trees above all
veining the grey
where the geese come in
haunting the dark
afternoon when the sky
pulls back with
the slow lap of Solway
seeping round pocks
of grass and thrift
where the marsh cows
threaten with their looks
and you want to get past
before they guess your fear
and the urgent breath frosts
with your heart.

Edgar considers a mortgage

They lay around me those
who I have loved, even
the one who cashed in my trust
for private gain. Pledged to death

their mortgage now is paid.
What need for me to guess
the span of years in which
I have a right to my own soul?

Capital might be gained,
some comfort in supposing
I have a tenure on my life
that will allow the heart

to heal, repair the misery
I bear, and with the wisdom
of some quiet years become
at peace with poor Tom.

Yet there's no guessing at events
or how our pretty thoughts
may still prove treasonous.
Tides kiss the walls

and seasons confute their rote.
I look in vain for idle things
to dandle in my mind, decide
to pocket what I know.

Edgar by the Gelt

It's wild today,
thrashes into groins that
turn its dissent
downstream, avoid
direct assault.
Boulders grumble beneath
breakers, white water
where once he soaked,
still, in the marrow cold
of summer night.
It troubles him this flux
of moods, watching.
His fingers green
with slime on ash.
Fungi burst through
the bark of fallen birch.
No chance of settling,
for nothing lasts
yet all's the same.
The squirrel is alert
to simple duties
and its necessary play.

I should be happy,
he thinks, for this is
a commonwealth
where I have a part,
can watch and maunder,
be particular at will
The politics of buzzard,
goldcrest, salmon, vole,
will not ensnare me.

Edgar takes an allotment

My patch for a time, this, allotted.
I will clear it of persistent menace –
twitch, dock and neighbouring nettle,
ground elder that Romans brought for salad.
I will pick each snip of broken root
for from neglect more vexation grows.
I'll light a fire that signals my intent,
smoulders with the efforts of my weeding,
comforts as I crouch on aching thighs
picking among unruly soil.
I have a palisade of corrugated iron
and stakes, know my estate's dimensions
as neighbours know theirs. My shed
is where I will prepare for proper husbandry,
the planting of sound stock
that will reward with crops
of known provenance.
Cinders, soot, my vigilance
will deter marauders that would infect
the core of all that's good.